Perfect Poems
for Teaching Phonics

By Deborah Ellermeyer and Judi Hechtman
with Sandra Ford Grove

Joyful LEARNING

NEW YORK • TORONTO • LONDON • AUCKLAND • SYDNEY
MEXICO CITY • NEW DELHI • HONG KONG • BUENOS AIRES

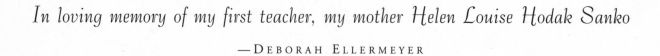

In loving memory of my first teacher, my mother Helen Louise Hodak Sanko

—DEBORAH ELLERMEYER

To my husband Mike, who encourages me to reach for the stars

—JUDI HECHTMAN

To my good friend Michelle Scanlan

—SANDRA FORD GROVE

Thanks to our students at The University School.
Their participation in sample lessons and enthusiasm
about poetry encouraged us to write this book.

"Catch a Little Rhyme" From *Catch A Little Rhyme* by Eve Merriam. Copyright © 1966 by Eve Merriam. Copyright renewed 1994 by Dee Michel and Guy Michel. Used by permission of Marian Reiner.

"Rainbow Paintbox" and "Seed, Sprout, Flower" by Helen H. Moore. Copyright © 1997 by Helen H. Moore.

"Pumpkin Pie Time" by Dorothy Jean Sklar. Copyright © 1998 by Dorothy Jean Sklar.

Home-School Consultant: Susan L. Lingo, Bright Ideas Books™
Edited by Wiley Blevins
Front cover design by Kathy Massaro and Diana Walters
Interior design by Kathy Massaro
Interior illustration by Tammie Lyon with additional artwork by Maxie Chambliss and James Graham Hale

ISBN 0439-40811-3

Contents

Poem	Phonics Focus	Theme	
EAT THE ALPHABET	alphabet recognition	*Food*	6
CATCH A LITTLE RHYME	rhyme	*Fantasy*	9
NATURE IS VERY BUSY	rhyme	*Nature*	14
BIG, BRIGHT CIRCUS	consonant /b/ *b*	*Circus*	17
WONDERFUL WEATHER	consonant /w/ *w*	*Weather*	20
RAINBOW PAINTBOX	consonant /r/ *r*	*Colors*	25
SMELLS OF SUMMER	consonant /s/ *s*	*Senses/Seasons*	28
CLOUDS	digraphs and blends	*Clouds*	31
SPIN, SPIDER, SPIN!	consonant blends	*Spiders*	35
DID YOU EVER GO FISHING?	long and short *a*	*Fish*	40
LEAF BLANKETS	long and short *e*	*Leaves & Trees*	44
PUMPKIN PIE TIME	long and short *i*	*Thanksgiving*	48
THE MORE IT SNOWS	long and short *o*	*Winter*	52
SEED, SPROUT, FLOWER	diphthongs	*Seeds & Plants*	55
FLASHLIGHTS IN THE DARK	compound words	*Insects*	59
FRIENDS	syllables	*Friendship*	62

Introduction

You probably know from firsthand experience that read-aloud poems are a surefire way to delight and instruct young children. Poems also offer great opportunities for the direct teaching of phonics. We have selected the poems in *Perfect Poems for Teaching Phonics* for their link to important phonics skills as well as for their playful appeal and connection to popular primary grade themes. With each illustrated reproducible poem, we have designated a key phonics skill to teach. Following each poem's introduction and phonics instruction, you will find several activities to extend learning and spark children's imagination. These language arts activities and games engage children in applying phonics skills and offer you opportunities to assess children's progress within authentic language contexts. And in "Poetry Corner," a feature that accompanies many of the lessons, you'll find suggestions for poetry collections that extend the lesson's theme.

We hope that these poems and related activities serve as models for additional ways you might use read-aloud poems in your classroom.

Enjoy!

How to Use This Book

To get the most instructional benefits from the poems, activities, and games in this book, we suggest the following:

☼ **Familiarize yourself with the phonics instruction provided.**

Browse through the book. Select a poem that fits your instructional needs. Note how we introduce the phonics skill. Consider any exceptions to the phonics principle being taught to ready yourself for the lesson.

☼ **Write the poems on chart paper and photocopy them for children.**

Use large print for easy viewing by children. You may wish to laminate the charts so you can write on and reuse them. Always read aloud the poem one or more times before inviting children to read it.

Also, make a copy of the poems for each child. Children will enjoy having their own copy of the poem to follow as you read aloud. After the lesson, they can read the poem independently or bring it home to share with family members. Consider having children make a collection of all of the poems in this book. Simply photocopy the poem pages, insert them between tagboard front and back covers, punch holes, and bind with brass fasteners or colorful ribbon or yarn.

Prepare lessons in advance of teaching.

Some lessons require minimal preparation. A list of materials and setup suggestions are provided with each poem.

Create learning centers using the activities and materials provided.

After introducing an activity or game, place the related materials in a learning center for independent child practice. This will provide additional opportunities to reinforce the phonics skill.

Use the following prompts and questions while children read to help them focus on and apply their knowledge of previously taught phonics skills.

- Find all of the words that [*begin/end*] with the letter _____.

- Pick a word and tell me what sound you hear at the [*beginning/end*].

- Find a word that [*begins/ends*] with the sound you hear at the [*beginning/end*] of _____.

- Find a word that rhymes with _____.

- How many words [*begin/end*] with the _____ sound? What are they?

- Find all the words that contain the _____ [*say a long or short vowel sound*] sound. This is the sound you hear in the word _____.

- Find all the words that begin with _____ [*say the sound(s) of a consonant blend or digraph*].

- Find a [*one syllable/two syllable/three syllable, etc.*] word.

- Find the word with the [*most/fewest*] syllables.

- Find a compound word. What two words make up this compound word?

Encourage children to interact with the poems.

As you read the poems with children, encourage them to anticipate upcoming rhymes, recite predictable portions, suggest word substitutions, and afterward, rewrite their own personalized versions of the poems.

Print shorter, predictable rhyming poems on sentence strips, numbering the back of each strip according to its sequence in the poem. Then invite children to put the sentence strips in order and to check their efforts.

Eat the Alphabet

A is **a**pple, **B** is **b**ean
C is **c**elery, fresh and green.

D is **d**oughnut, **E** is **e**gg
F is **f**ig, rolling down your leg!

G is **g**rapefruit, **H** is **h**oney,
I is **i**ce cream, soft and runny.

J is **j**ello, **K** is **k**nish,
L is **l**ettuce, and **l**ic-o-rice!

M is **m**eatball, **N** is **n**ut,
O is **o**range, peeled or cut!

P is **p**izza, **Q** is **q**uince,
R is **r**ice fit for a prince!

S is **s**paghetti, **T** is **t**angerine,
U is **u**pside-down cake with cream between.

V is **v**egetable soup, **W** is **w**affle,
X is scrambled **x** (Isn't that joke awful!)

Y is **y**ogurt, **Z** is **z**ucchini,
Let's eat the alphabet on a bed of linguine!

by Meish Goldish

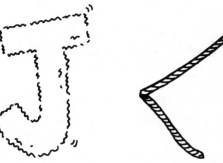

Eat the Alphabet

Setup

- Photocopy the poem on page 6 for each child and write the poem on chart paper. Highlight each upper- and lowercase letter pair by printing them in the same color marker or underlining them.

- On each index card, print an uppercase letter on the left-hand side and the corresponding lowercase letter on the right-hand side.

- Cut each index card in half in unique ways to create puzzle pieces.

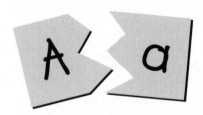

SKILL

alphabet recognition

Materials

- chart paper
- markers
- scissors
- 26 large index cards
- pointer
- grocery bag

Using the Poem

1 Ask children to name their favorite foods. List their responses on the chalkboard or chart paper, and underline the first letter in each food name.

2 Explain to children that you are going to read an ABC poem that names a food for each letter of the alphabet. Track the print with a pointer as you read the poem. Challenge children to listen carefully to see if the name of their favorite food is included.

3 When completed, do the following: Give each child an index card puzzle piece containing an uppercase letter. One at a time, ask children to identify the letter on their puzzle piece and find it in the poem. Ask children if they know any other foods that begin with that letter.

4 Have children arrange the uppercase puzzle pieces in alphabetical order on the floor.

5 Place the lowercase letter puzzle pieces in a grocery bag. Tell children that they will be going shopping for lowercase letters to match the uppercase letters on the floor. Have each child choose a puzzle piece from the grocery bag. Ask the child to identify the letter on the puzzle piece and find its corresponding uppercase match on the floor. After playing, you may wish to place the puzzle pieces in a learning center for children to use during center time.

Poetry Corner

Eating the Alphabet Bulletin Board

Read aloud *Eating the Alphabet* by Lois Ehlert (Harcourt Brace, 1989). Let children compare it with the poem. Then review the names of the fruits and vegetables included. Assign each child a letter of the alphabet, or have each child choose a favorite letter such as the first letter in his or her name. Have children write the upper- and lowercase form of the letter on a piece of construction paper and add drawings or paste magazine pictures of foods whose names begin with that letter. Display these in alphabetical order on a bulletin board. For children experiencing difficulty, have them draw the foods mentioned in *Eating the Alphabet* for their letter.

Extend this activity by placing a collection of alphabet books in a learning center. Discuss with children the various themes chosen by the authors and illustrators. Then provide materials for children to create their own alphabet books. Encourage children to work with partners or in small groups. Place the completed books in the classroom library.

ABC Order

Discuss with children the concept of alphabetizing words. Provide several examples on the chalkboard, using the names of common foods such as *apple, banana,* and *carrot.* Choose words that do not have the same first letter. Then have children form several small groups. Write the names of the fruits and vegetables in *Eating the Alphabet* on small index cards, and give each group three or four fruit name cards to arrange in alphabetical order. You may wish to have groups exchange cards for further practice.

Catch a Little Rhyme

Once upon a time
I caught a little rhyme

I set it on the floor
but it ran right out the door

I chased it on my bicycle
but it melted to an icicle

I scooped it up in my hat
but it turned into a cat

I caught it by the tail
but it stretched into a whale

I followed it in a boat
but it changed into a goat

When I fed it tin and paper
it became a tall skyscraper

Then it grew into a kite
and flew far out of sight...

by Eve Merriam

Catch a Little Rhyme

Materials

☼ chart paper
☼ markers
☼ sentence strips
☼ paper and pencils

Setup

● Photocopy the poem on page 9 for each child and write the poem on chart paper.

● Write the following "hink pinks" on sentence strips. (Hink pinks are riddles whose answers consist of two one-syllable rhyming words.) Write the answer to each on the back of the sentence strip.

What do you call a large hog? (big pig)
What do you call a small, pretend body of water? (fake lake)
What do you call a little walkway in a house? (small hall)
What do you call useful lumber? (good wood)

Using the Poem

1 Discuss with children the concept of rhyme. Begin by stating two words that rhyme (for example, *bat/sat*) and modeling why they rhyme. For example, you might say, "The words *bat* and *sat* rhyme because they sound the same at the end. They both end in /at/. Do you know any other words that rhyme with *bat* and *sat*?"

2 Have children suggest rhyming word pairs. Write the word pairs on the chalkboard. It might be necessary to point out that some rhyming word pairs don't have the same spelling pattern (for example, *sun/one*).

3 Now read aloud the poem. Ask children to listen for rhyming words. After reading, have children circle rhyming word pairs.

4 Next, introduce children to hink pinks. Display each of the hink pink sentence strips. Help children to solve the riddles. Then challenge children to write their own hink pinks. Suggest that they begin by writing a rhyming word pair, then thinking of a riddle to go with the rhyme.

5 For an additional challenge, have children write hinkie pinkies (riddles whose answers consist of two two-syllable rhyming words) or hinkety pinketies (riddles whose answers consist of two three-syllable rhyming words).

Rhyme Concentration

Have children play Rhyme Concentration. Make a copy of the Rhyme Concentration game cards on pages 12–13. Paste the cards onto small index cards for added durability. Mix up the cards and spread them out facedown on a table or floor. In turn, each player turns over two cards and states aloud the picture names. If the two picture names rhyme, the player gets to keep the cards. If the card names do not rhyme, the player turns the cards over in their original position. The object of the game is to remember where cards are located so that pairs can be formed in future turns. Each player continues in turn until all the pairs have been found. The player with the most cards at the end of the game wins.

The Rhyming Circle

Have children sit in a circle on the floor. State aloud a word that has many rhyming words. You may wish to use one of the words listed below. The child to the right of you says your word and a rhyming word. The game continues as each child in the circle gets a turn. Play continues until no more rhyming words can be found. You may wish to continue with other words and rhymes.

Rhyming Circle Starter Words

back	best	chin	gum	more
bad	bring	clock	hair	rash
bake	broom	cries	joke	ride
ball	bun	cut	lend	right
band	burn	day	less	sail
base	can	drink	lip	shop
bean	car	feet	made	tank
bed	cat	gate	mice	train
bee	cheer	good	mine	wild
bent	chew	grow	mix	

Rhyme Concentration
Game Cards

Perfect Poems for Teaching Phonics   Joyful Learning

Rhyme Concentration
Game Cards

Nature Is Very Busy

Bees are buzzing, frogs are hopping,
　　Moles are digging. There's no stopping
Vines from climbing, grass from growing,
　　Birds from singing, winds from blowing,
Buds from blooming, crickets humming
　　Sunbeams dancing, raindrops drumming.
All the world is whirling, dizzy
　　Nature is very busy!

by Frances Gorman Risser

Nature Is Very Busy

Setup

● Photocopy the poem on page 14 for each child and write the poem on chart paper.

Using the Poem

1 Ask children to list words that describe things in nature (weather, animals, plants, and so on). On chart paper or the chalkboard, record their responses on a nature word web such as the one shown. Then explain to children that you are going to read a poem about nature. Read aloud "Nature Is Very Busy," and allow time for children to share their responses to the poem.

2 Ask children to locate in the poem words that end in *-ing*. Point out that these words are called verbs, or action words. Invite volunteers to circle each *-ing* rhyming word pair.

3 Then have children create their own "Nature Is Very Busy" book by following the same format as the poem. Begin by having them look at the word web they created earlier. Invite them to create new webs, using action words, for different categories. For example, after reading the poem, children might want to create a separate web to describe the way different animals move, the sounds they make, and so on, or a web that describes water in different ways. Be sure to include *-ing* words in the webs.

4 When the webs are completed, have children form small groups. Assign each group a category (animals, plants, weather, and so on). Invite each group to write a poem using as many rhyming *-ing* words as possible. Groups can also illustrate their poems. Then collect the poems and bind them into a book titled "Nature Is Very Busy" book."

Materials

※ chart paper
※ markers
※ paper and pencils
※ crayons
※ tagboard
※ hole punch
※ brass fasteners or string

Poetry Corner

Explore the busy world of nature and the changing seasons with the lively and lyrical poems in *Voices on the Wind: Poems for All Seasons*, selected by David Booth (Morrow Junior Books, 1990). Soft, lyrical paintings complement each poem.

In *Just Around the Corner: Poems About the Seasons* (Henry Holt, 1993), poet Leland Jacobs celebrates the seasons with 25 playful poems about autumn leaves, tracks in the snow, spring rain, and more. The bold, colorful collage illustrations will invite young readers to visit this collection again and again.

Action Word Pantomime

Play Action Word Pantomime. Write an *-ing* word on each of 35 index cards. You may wish to use these and other action words: *bowling, clapping, combing, crying, dancing, digging, drawing, driving, eating, falling, flying, hopping, hugging, juggling, jumping, kicking, mixing, mopping, painting, playing, raking, reading, running, singing, skating, skipping, sleeping, smelling, spilling, sweeping, swimming, swaying, waving, writing, yawning*. Place the cards in a bag. Have a volunteer select a card from the bag and pantomime the action word written on it. Challenge the class to identify the word. Continue until all children have had an opportunity to pantomime a word.

Growing Verbs

Help children identify the root word in words that end in the suffix *-ing*. Write the word *eating* on the board. Invite a child to underline the root word. Let children suggest other words that end in *-ing* and repeat this process. Then, using the illustration below as a guide, help children make word pull-throughs using large index cards, paper, and scissors.

Big, Bright Circus

The circus is
big,
    bright,
        brilliant,
            breathtaking;
beautiful,
    bobbing,
        bouncy,
            bustling;
blue,
    bliss,
        beaming,
            booming;
blooming,
    blazing,
        bubbly,
            buzzing,
                BURSTING!

by Mary Anne Magnan

17

Big, Bright Circus

Materials

☼ chart paper
☼ marker

Setup

● Photocopy the poem on page 17 for each child and write the poem on chart paper.

Using the Poem

1 Read aloud the poem. Ask children what sound they hear at the beginning of most of the poem words—/b/. Say /b/ and ask children to repeat it. Point out that the letter *b* stands for this sound. Then point to a *b* word in the poem and have volunteers identify a circus object that could be described by the word (for example, big tent, bright lights, breathtaking performances).

2 Explain to children that they will be writing a class poem using "Big, Bright Circus" as a model. Discuss possible poem topics with children and have them choose their favorite. Then have children brainstorm a list of possible *b* words that could be used to describe the topic. List these words on the chalkboard. Have children use these words as you write the poem together.

3 You may wish to have children work in pairs or small groups to create additional poems. Children may wish to focus on letters other than *b* for these poems.

Scattegories

Play a version of the game Scattegories using categories that require *b*-word responses. For example, if the category is Summer Activities, players have one minute to think of *b* words or phrases to fit this category. Possible responses might include *blowing bubbles, beach trip, bouncing a ball, basketball, boating,* and *biking.* Begin play by stating a category such as Games. Allow one minute for children to record their responses. Players then share their responses. If two or more players have the same response, the responses are stricken and no points are awarded. A point is scored for each unique response only. Repeat the procedure with new categories such as Things You Eat, Television Shows, Things You Wear, Things You Take on a Vacation, and Things Found in Our Classroom.

I Spy

Play I Spy. Have children identify objects whose names begin with *b*. For example, you might say, "I spy something in the classroom that is rectangular. Its name begins with /b/." Children offer guesses. If necessary, provide additional clues such as, "This rectangular object is about 12 inches long and 6 inches wide. It contains words and pictures." Once the correct object is named (book), continue with other objects and clues.

Poetry Corner

Delightful, colorful illustrations enhance Jack Prelutsky's playful verses about the big top in *Circus* (Simon & Schuster, 1989).

Wonderful Weather

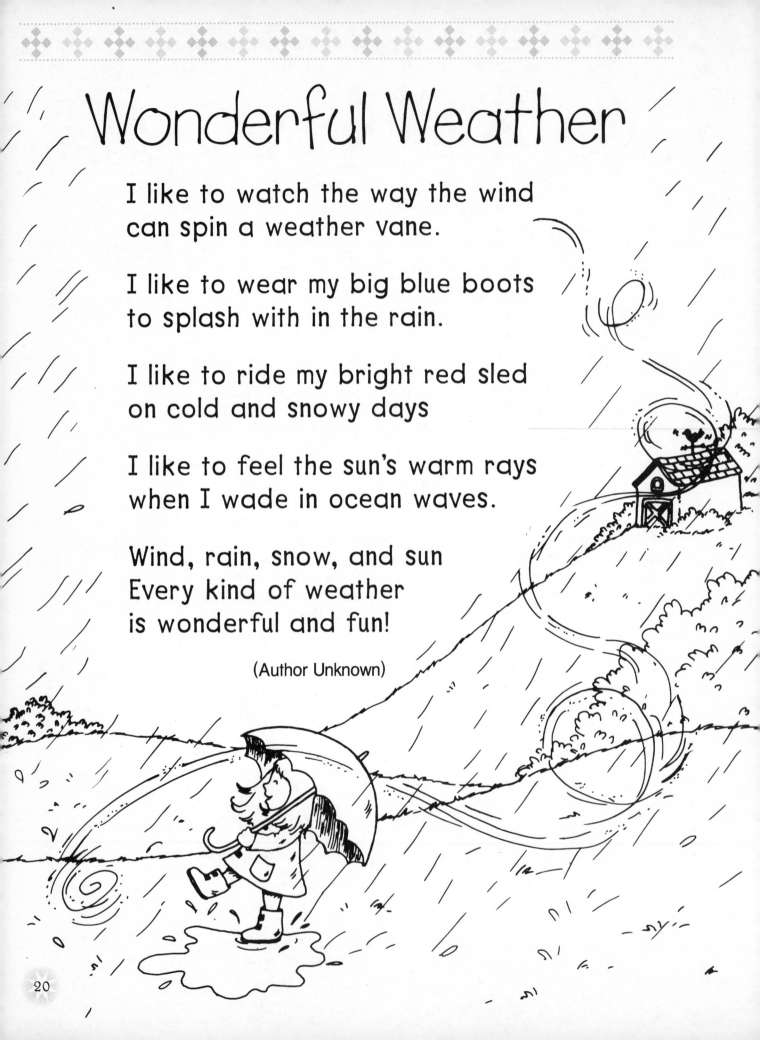

I like to watch the way the wind
can spin a weather vane.

I like to wear my big blue boots
to splash with in the rain.

I like to ride my bright red sled
on cold and snowy days

I like to feel the sun's warm rays
when I wade in ocean waves.

Wind, rain, snow, and sun
Every kind of weather
is wonderful and fun!

(Author Unknown)

Wonderful Weather

Setup

- Photocopy the poem on page 20 for each child and write the poem on chart paper.

- Make copies of the windmill pattern for each child.

Using the Poem

1. Read aloud the poem's title, emphasizing the initial sound—/w/. Ask children to list weather-related words that begin with /w/, such as *windy* and *warm*. Challenge them to listen for words with /w/ as you read aloud the poem.

2. Distribute a copy of the windmill pattern to each child. Ask children to write words that begin with /w/ on each blank line. Then invite them to color both sides and cut along the dotted lines.

3. Show children how to make their windmills. Place the pattern on a piece of folded newspaper. Then bring each corner with a star into the center so that the stars all line up, one on top of another. Help children poke a pushpin through the stars, being careful not to crease the paper blades. Then they can insert the pin into the side of a pencil eraser.

PUSHPIN THROUGH ERASER

4. Invite children to share the words on their Wonderful *W* Windmills with classmates. Then go outside, catch a breeze, and see the windmills turn!

Materials

- chart paper
- markers
- windmill pattern (page 23)
- crayons
- scissors
- pencils with erasers
- newspaper
- pushpins

Poetry Corner

Weather, poems selected by Lee Bennett Hopkins (HarperCollins, 1994). Beginning readers will enjoy these short verses about wind, rain, snow, and sun by noted poets Lilian Moore, David McCord, Charlotte Zolotow, and others.

W Wishing Well

Construct a simple wishing well out of an oatmeal box, craft sticks, and construction paper. Inside the well, place a variety of pictures or small objects whose names begin with /w/. You may wish to use the picture cards on page 24. Then have volunteers select a picture or item from the wishing well and describe it for the class to guess its identity. For example, if a watermelon picture card is selected, the child might say, "I am wishing for a large fruit. This fruit is green on the outside and red on the inside. It's name begins with /w/. What is it?" The child who correctly guesses the picture or item's identity is the next to draw from the well.

Special Pebbles

Read aloud *Sylvester and the Magic Pebble* by William Steig (Simon & Schuster, 1988). Ask children what they would wish or hope for if they found a special pebble. Then give each child a sheet of heavy construction paper. Let children glue a "special pebble" to the top of the paper. (You might use real pebbles or beans painted red for your "special pebbles.") Ask children to write a brief story about their wishes or hopes, using as many words as possible that begin with /w/. Attach the stories to the bottom of the construction paper, and invite children to illustrate them. They may wish to incorporate the pebbles into their illustrations.

Windmill Pattern

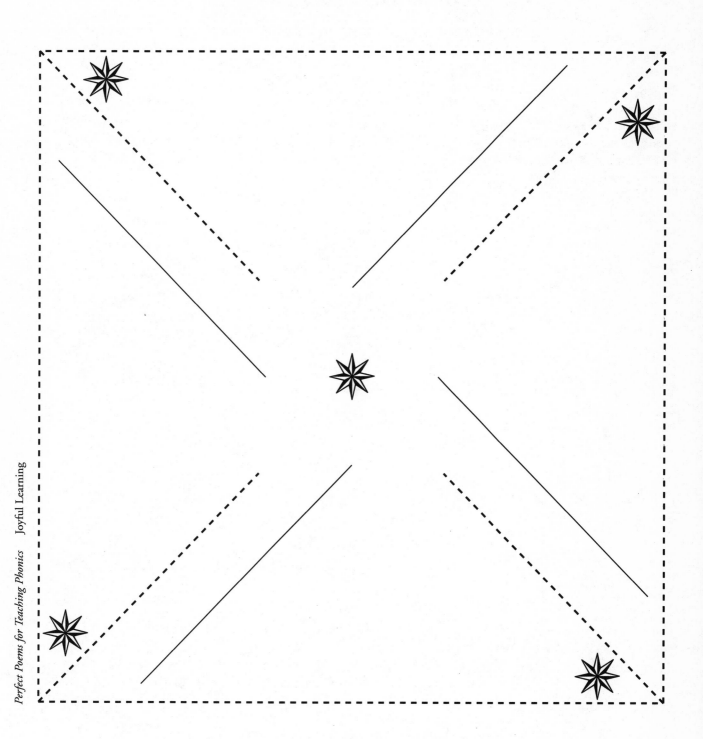

Wishing Well

Picture Cards

Perfect Poems for Teaching Phonics Joyful Learning

Rainbow Paintbox

I can see a rainbow,
when the rain has gone away.
All the colors of the rainbow
I can name them all for you today:

Red there is, a rosy red, a red so bright and bonny,
and orange as a tiger lily, so bold and tawny,

yellow as the blazing sun, that gives us all our light,
and green as grass beneath our feet,
blue as the sky so bright.

There's indigo, as dark as night,
and violet like flowers.

These are the colors nature paints
the sky with
after showers.

by Helen H. Moore

Rainbow Paintbox

Materials

* chart paper
* markers
* construction paper (in the colors of the rainbow)
* scissors
* brown paper bag
* tape
* rainbow picture

Setup

* Photocopy the poem on page 25 for each child and write the poem on chart paper. You may wish to write the color words using the appropriate color marker.

* Cut out 35 construction paper word cards—5 red, 5 orange, 5 yellow, 5 green, 5 blue, 5 indigo, and 5 violet. Cut each card into an arc shape, about the size of a small index card. Write the following words on the construction paper word cards: *rabbit, race, rag, rain, rake, ranch, rat, ray, rain, red, rent, ride, rip, road, rock, room, rose, rope, rug, run, bear, car, chair, deer, door, finger, four, her, jar, ladder, letter, pear, spider, zipper, hear.* Be sure that each colored word card set contains at least two words that begin or end with /r/.

* Make the "pot at the end of the rainbow." Cut out a pot from black construction paper and attach it to the front of a brown paper bag. Place the colored word cards in the bag.

Using the Poem

1 Display a picture of a rainbow. Spark discussion by asking questions such as "What is this?" "When is a rainbow usually seen?" "What colors are present in a rainbow?" "Are the colors always in the same order?" Share with children the acronym ROY G. BIV. Point out that this name is a simple way to remember the colors of the rainbow in the order in which they always appear (from the top of the arc to the bottom: **Red, Orange, Yellow, Green, Blue, Indigo, Violet**).

2 Then read aloud the poem. Ask children to listen for words that begin with /r/ as in *rainbow*. After reading, have children underline words in the poem that begin with /r/.

3 Tell children that they will be creating rainbows using colored word cards. Divide the class into five teams. Have one member of each team select a colored word card from the "pot." If the card contains a word that begins with /r/, the team must read it aloud and place it on the desk in the appropriate place it appears in the rainbow. For example, if the team chooses a red card with the word *rat*, the team would place the card on the top portion of the rainbow. Play continues until one team has formed an *r* rainbow. Then collect the cards and play again.

4 You may wish to repeat the procedure, asking children to create *r* rainbows using words that end with /r/.

Row Your Boat

To further reinforce the /r/ sound, write the song "Row Your Boat" on chart paper. Have children circle all the words that contain /r/. Discuss with children whether this sound appears in the initial, medial, or final position in each word. Then have children sing the song while making a rowing motion. You may wish to sing the song in rounds.

Row Your Boat

Row, row, row your boat
Gently down the stream,
Merrily, merrily, merrily, merrily—
Life is but a dream.

During later singings, challenge children to add verses to the song. These verses should include other action words that begin with /r/. Invite children to perform the accompanying actions. Possible verses include:

- Rub, rub, rub your hands.
- Race, race, race your car.
- Reach, reach, reach your arms.
- Rake, rake, rake your leaves.
- Read, read, read your book.
- Raise, raise, raise your hands.

Recycle It

Write the word *recycle* on the chalkboard. Ask children what the word means (to use again). Have children repeat the word, extending the initial /r/. Then invite children to create robots out of recycled cardboard boxes, paper towel tubes, cloth, aluminum foil, buttons, pipe cleaners, soda cans, Styrofoam meat trays, and any other available materials. Encourage children to give their robots names that begin with /r/ such as Ralph the Really Rad Recycled Robot, Roger the Ridiculous Recycled Robot, or Rosie the Ravishing Recycled Robot.

Poetry Corner

Invite children to compare the quartet of poems titled "Four Poems for Roy G Biv" in Barbara Juster Esbenson's *Who Shrank My Grandmother's House? Poems of Discovery* (HarperCollins, 1992). Each poem explores rainbows from a different poetic perspective.

Hailstones & Halibut Bones: Adventures in Color by Mary O'Neill (Doubleday, 1989). Exuberant, colorful illustrations accompany 12 sensory-rich poems about colors in this revised edition of the 1961 classic.

Smells of Summer

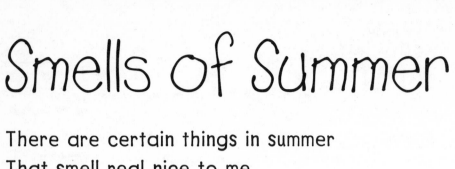

There are certain things in summer
That smell real nice to me.
The moss and ferns and woodsy things
I like especially.

The grassy lawn just freshly cut,
The fragrant stacks of hay,
The clean outdoors when it has rained,
The salty ocean spray—

Pine needles warming in the sun,
Fresh corn, and berries, too,
Bright flowers in a big bouquet—
I like these smells, don't you?

by Vivian Gouled

etry
orner

"Bumblebee"
mmer Stars,"
een Fisher
es the sights
sounds of
ner in *Out in*
Dark and
ht (Harper &
, 1980), a
rical and
ical collection
ems about
ch of the
easons.

Share a Secret

Have children sit in a circle. Then whisper a secret message into the ear of the child sitting to your right. The message should contain a number of words that begin with /s/. For example, "I see seven silly sisters sitting in the sand." The child who receives the message should pass it along by whispering it into the ear of the classmate sitting to his or her right. The message continues to be passed around the circle. The last child repeats the message aloud, and the class compares it to the original message. The game continues with a new secret message.

S Musical Chairs

Play a version of Musical Chairs, but instead of playing music, have children circle around the chairs while you say a list of words. When they hear a word that begins with /s/, they must try to find a seat.

Smells of Summer

Setup

● Photocopy the poem on page 28 for each child and write the poem on chart paper.

● Write the following tongue twisters on chart paper:

Sally sells seashells by the seashore.
Sammy slurps seven sodas on a sunny Saturday.
Sarah smiles silly smiles sitting on some slimy seals.

Using the Poem

1 Tell children that they are going on an imaginary trip. Ask them to close their eyes and imagine the following scenario. Encourage them to use their senses to imagine the sights and sounds described. Tell them that they will share what they remember about the trip.

It is a hot summer day. The sunshine is streaming down on your shoulders. You are walking on a sandy beach. You can smell the saltwater in the air. You see seagulls soaring above. Around you are swimmers, surfers, and sailboats. You hear sandals slapping on the boardwalk. You see people in swimsuits. Children are playing in the sand. Thirsty sunbathers are sipping sodas. Slowly the sun sinks into the horizon and a summer night begins.

2 Ask children to open their eyes to return from the trip. Invite them to recall the things that they saw, heard, felt, smelled, and tasted. Write their recollections on the chalkboard. Underline words and phrases that begin with /s/ as you record their memories. Call children's attention to the /s/ at the beginning of these words.

3 Read aloud the poem "Smells of Summer." Ask children to listen for words that begin with /s/.

4 Discuss with children their favorite season. Have them share sights, sounds, feelings, smells, and tastes common to their favorite season.

5 Display the chart paper containing the tongue twisters. Read them aloud and provide time for children to practice saying them. Challenge children to create a tongue twister using the /s/ sound to describe their favorite season. For example, to describe winter: *Sarita slides smoothly on her sled in the slippery snow.*

Clouds

White sheep, white sheep
On a blue hill,
When the wind stops
You all stand still.
When the wind blows
You walk away slow.
White sheep, white sheep,
Where do you go?

by Christina G. Rossetti

Clouds

Materials

- chart paper
- markers
- self-sticking notes

Setup

● Photocopy the poem on page 31 for each child and write the poem on chart paper.

Using the Poem

1 Write on the chalkboard a list of common consonant blends such as *bl, cl, fl, gl, sl, br, cr, dr, fr, gr, pr, sc, sm, sn, sp,* and *st.* Model how to blend each letter pair. Point out that each sound in a consonant blend is heard. Ask children to generate words that begin with each blend. List these words on the chalkboard. Then explain to children that the poem "Clouds" contains several words that begin with these common sounds. Read aloud the poem and ask children to add these words to the lists on the chalkboard.

2 During a later reading, focus on the many consonant digraphs in the poem. Explain to children that sometimes when two consonants appear together in a word they stand for a sound that is different from either sound individually or combined. List common digraphs on the chalkboard such as *wh, ch, sh,* and *th.* Model the sound that each digraph stands for, and ask children to generate words that begin with these sounds. List these words on the chalkboard. Then reread the poem, and ask children to listen for words that begin with these sounds. Add these words to the lists.

3 Ask children to select words on the lists that could be used as substitutes for the poem words *white* or *sheep* (for example, <u>bl</u>ack <u>wh</u>ale). Write these words on self-sticking notes, place them in the appropriate places in the poem, and have children chorally read the new poem.

What's in the Cloud? Mobile

Read aloud *It Looked Like Spilt Milk* by Charles Shaw (HarperCollins, 1988). Have children select an object whose name begins with a consonant digraph or blend, then make the object by gluing cotton balls to construction paper. Have children label their cloud-shaped pictures "White [name of the object]." Then tape a long piece of string to each picture and hang from the ceiling.

Cloud Game

Make multiple copies of the cloud patterns on page 34. Paste the patterns to construction paper squares or index cards. On the back of each cloud write a word that begins with a consonant blend or digraph. You may wish to use the words below. Small groups of three or four children can play the game. To play, one child selects a card and reads aloud the word on the back. If the word is correctly read, the child keeps the card. If not, the card is placed on the bottom of the pile. Play continues until all words have been correctly read.

Digraphs

ch: chain, chair, check, cheese, chest, chew, child, chill, chin, chop, chug, churn, beach, branch, each, lunch, peach, such, teach

sh: shade, shake, shape, shark, sharp, she, sheep, shell, ship, shoe, shop, show, shut, brush, cash, dish, fish, fresh, push, rush, trash, wash, wish

th: thank, thermos, thick, thin, thing, think, third, thorn, three, throw, thumb, bath, both, math, moth, path, teeth, with

wh: whale, what, wheel, when, where, which, while, whisper, white, whiz, why

Blends

br: brain, brake, branch, brave, bread, break, brick, bridge, bring, broom, brush

cr: crab, crack, crane, crash, creek, crib, crop, cross, crown, crunch, cry

dr: dragon, drain, drank, draw, dream, dress, drink, drip, drive, drop, drum, dry

fr: frame, free, freeze, fresh, friend, frog, from, front, fruit, fry

gr: grab, grade, grape, grass, gray, great, green, grew, grin, group, grumpy

pr: pray, prank, pretty, press, price, pride, print, problem, project, prop, prune

tr: track, trade, train, trap, trash, tray, treat, tree, trip, troop, truck, true, try

bl: black, blame, blank, bleed, blind, block, blow, blue

cl: clam, clap, class, claw, clay, clean, cliff, clip, close, cloud, club

fl: flag, flame, flash, flat, flee, flight, flip, float, floor, flower, fluff, flu, fly

gl: glad, glass, gleam, glide, globe, glove, glow, glue

pl: place, plan, plane, planet, plate, please, plenty, pliers, plot, plow, plug

sl: slam, sled, sleep, sleeve, slice, slide, slip, slow, slug, slumber

sc: scale, scar, scare, scarf, scoop, scout, sculpt

sk: skate, sketch, ski, skid, skill, skin, skip, skit, skunk

sm: small, smart, smash, smear, smell, smile, smoke, smuggle

sn: snack, snail, snake, snap, sneeze, snip, sniff, snow, snoop, snug

sp: space, spark, speak, speech, speed, spell, spend, spill, spoon, sport, spurt

st: stack, stage, stamp, stand, star, start, state, step, stick, still, stop, store, stun

sw: swan, swap, sweat, sweep, swell, swim, swing, swoop

Poetry Corner

Explore sky phenomena such as clouds, shooting meteors, and the stars with *Sky Worlds* (Macmillan, 1994), a collection of poems by Marilyn Singer. Lovely paintings evoke the mood of each poem.

Cloud Patterns

Perfect Poems for Teaching Phonics   Joyful Learning

Spin, Spider, Spin!

Spin, spider, spin!
Spin your web round and wide.
Spin your silky web with pride.
Greet the guests who come inside.
Spin, spider, spin!

by Meish Goldish

Spin, Spider, Spin

SKILL

consonant blends

Materials

- ☀ chart paper
- ☀ markers
- ☀ spiderweb wheel pattern (page 38)
- ☀ paper plates
- ☀ brass fasteners
- ☀ scissors
- ☀ pencils or crayons

Setup

⬤ Photocopy the poem on page 35 for each child and write the poem on chart paper.

Using the Poem

1 Ask children if they have ever seen a spider in its web. Have them share their observations. Then read aloud the poem. When finished, write the word *spider* on the chalkboard, underline the letters *sp*, and pronounce the consonant blend. Point out that both /s/ and /p/ are heard in this blend.

2 Have children search the poem for words that begin with the *sp*-blend. List these words on the chalkboard. Then ask children to add other words that begin with the *sp*-blend.

3 Give each child a copy of the spiderweb wheel pattern, a paper plate, brass fastener, and scissors. Have children cut out their wheel and center it on the plate. Then help them poke a brass fastener through the dot on the wheel and through the plate.

4 Have children turn the wheel and write words beginning with the *sp*-blend on the plate. Completed wheels can be placed in a learning center for individual practice by other children.

Slot or Stop *S*-Blend Game

After exploring the *sp*-blend, challenge children to come up with words that begin with other *s*-blends such as *sc, sk, sl, sm, sn, st,* and *sw.* Then play the Slot or Stop Game. Make a copy of the *s*-blend pictures on page 39 for each pair of children. Have children cut out the pictures, mix them up, and place them in a pile facedown. The first player calls out either "slot" or "stop." That player then chooses a picture card from the top of the pile and reads the name out loud. If it begins with the same sound as the word that was called out, the player keeps the card. If not, the player returns the card to the bottom of the pile. A "free" card may be used to match either "slot" or "stop." The winner is the player who has the most cards at the end of the game.

Silly *S*-Blend Stories

Choose an *s*-blend and challenge children to come up with a list of words that begin with the blend. Then invite the class to create a silly collaborative story with the words on the list. To help children begin, write a story starter on the board for the *st*-blend; for example, *Once upon a time, there was a starfish who had a sticky stone. One day…* Then ask volunteers to offer a phrase or sentence that continues the story and has at least one word with the target *s*-blend.

Poetry Corner

Flit, Flutter, Fly!: Poems About Bugs and Other Crawly Creatures, selected by Lee Bennett Hopkins (Doubleday, 1992), is a poetry collection custom-made for choral reading. Inviting illustrations enhance these 29 "buggy" tributes by Myra Cohn Livingston, Karla Kuskin, Aileen Fisher, and other favorite poets.

Spiderweb Wheel Pattern

Sp

Slot or Stop
Picture Cards

  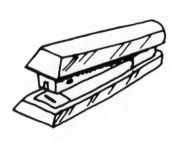

FREE

 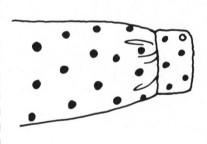 
FREE

Did You Ever Go Fishing?

Did you ever go fishing on a bright sunny day—
Sit on a fence and have the fence give way?
Slide off the fence and rip your pants,
And see the little fishes do the hokey-pokey dance?

(Author Unknown)

Did You Ever Go Fishing?

Setup

- Photocopy the poem on page 40 for each child and write the poem on chart paper.

- Make multiple copies of the fish patterns. Cut out each pattern. On the back of each fish write one of the following short- or long-vowel *a* words: *am, back, bad, bat, can, cat, class, fast, hand, has, lamp, mad, math, rat, sad, stand, track, bake, came, face, lake, made, race, tape, mail, sail, train, wait, day, may, play, stay, tray, way.* When completed, attach a paper clip to each fish. Place the fish in a box or plastic tub to create a fish pond.

- To make a fishing rod, use a two-foot length of yarn to hang a small ring magnet from the end of each dowel.

- Write "long *a*" on one paper bag and "short *a*" on the other.

SKILL

long and short vowel *a*

Materials

- chart paper
- markers
- fish patterns (page 43)
- scissors
- paper clips
- plastic tub or box
- yarn
- small ring magnets
- 1/2-inch-wide dowel rods, about 1 foot long
- 2 paper bags

Using the Poem

1. Explain to children that a fish tale is a story in which the storyteller has exaggerated facts or events. This type of story got its name from fishermen who often exaggerated about the size of the fish they caught. Point out that the poem "Did You Ever Go Fishing?" contains an exaggeration (fish dancing the hokey-pokey). Encourage children to listen for this as you read aloud the poem.

2. Reread the poem with children. Have them locate words that have the letter *a*. Ask children to sort the words into two groups—one group containing words with /ă/ (short *a*), the other containing words with /ā/ (long *a*).

3. Next, explain to children that they will have an opportunity to "fish" for long- and short-*a* words in the fish pond. Fish are caught by passing the magnet near a paper clip. Once a fish is caught, have the child remove it from the pole and read aloud the word written on it. Ask the class to place the fish in the long-*a* or short-*a* bag according to the sound the word contains. Continue until all the fish are "caught." You may wish to place the game in a learning center for additional practice.

Poetry Corner

In the Swim: Poems and Paintings by Doug Florian (Harcourt Brace, 1997) includes 21 irresistible poems about salmon, sea horses, jellyfish, and other creatures of the deep, which children will clamor to read again and again.

Create a Fish

Read aloud *The Underwater Alphabet Book* by Jerry Pallotta (Charlesbridge Publishing, 1991). Discuss the many unusual fish it contains. Invite children to create imaginary fish using colored construction paper, sequins, glitter, colored cellophane, foil, and other craft materials. Then ask them to create a long- or short-*a* name for their fish (for example, Racing Rainbow Fish or Flat Fan Fish).

Grade A Collages

Have children cut out magazine pictures of objects whose names contain the long- or short-*a* sound. Children may wish to work in small groups to collect the pictures. When completed, have children sort the pictures into two piles—long *a* and short *a*. Then ask them to create collages using the pictures in each pile. Provide groups with large sheets of colored construction paper and glue. Each group should create two collages—a long-*a* collage and a short-*a* collage. Display the completed collages on a bulletin board.

Fish Patterns

Leaf Blankets

Leaves are falling, soft as snowflakes,
Red and yellow, gold and brown;
The breeze laughs gaily in the treetops,
Shaking all the color down.

Leaves are covering the gardens
As my blanket covers me.
When cold winter comes, the flowers
Will be warm as warm can be.

by Irene B. Crofoot

Leaf Blankets

Setup

* Photocopy the poem on page 44 for each child and write the poem on chart paper.

* On a bulletin board, construct a large tree that has at least eight branches, using the brown construction paper. On each branch write one of the following long- or short-*e* spelling patterns (phonograms): *ed, ell, est, et, e, eat, ee, eep.*

* Photocopy and cut out the leaf patterns, then use them to trace and cut out red, yellow, and orange construction paper leaves. Write the following words on the leaves, one per leaf: *bed, red, sled, bell, sell, tell, best, rest, west, wet, set, met, be, she, we, heat, meat, treat, bee, see, tree, sleep, deep, sheep.*

Using the Poem

1 Read aloud the poem. Ask children to listen for words that contain /ē/ for long *e* as in *leaf.* When completed, list these words on the chalkboard in separate columns. Have children add other words that belong to each word family. For example, *be* and *me* are in the same word family because they contain the same long-*e* spelling pattern.

2 Repeat step 1 for words with /ĕ/ as in *red.*

3 Show children the paper tree with the long- and short-*e* spelling patterns written on individual branches. Place the leaf word cards in a small trash bag. Have volunteers pick a leaf from the bag and tape it to the tree branch that contains the same spelling pattern. For example, the leaf card for *red* would be placed on the branch containing *ed.* If correct, the child can tape the leaf on its branch. Continue until all the leaves have been correctly attached to the tree. Provide blank leaves for children to add other words they encounter as they read.

Additional Long- and Short-*e* Spelling Patterns

Long *e*: *ea, each, ead, eak, eal, eam, ean, eap, ear, ease, east, eath, eave, eech, eed, eek, eel, eem, een, eet, eeze*

Short *e*: *eck, edge, eg, elt, em, en, ence, ench, end, ent, ess*

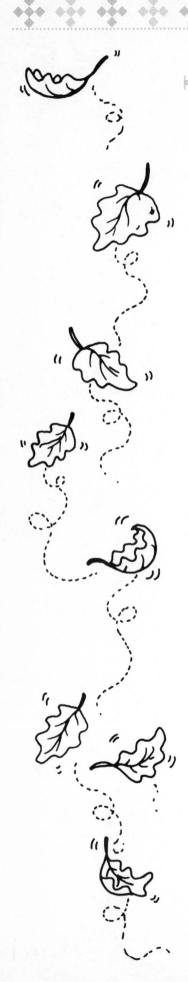

Word Family Flip Books

Let children create word family flip books. Provide each child with a piece of 2- by 10-inch posterboard. Have them write a long- or short-*e* spelling pattern (phonogram) on the right-hand side of the board. Punch a hole in the top, left-hand side of the posterboard. Then give children pieces of 2- by 4-inch white construction paper cards with a hole punched at the top. Make sure these holes align with the hole in the posterboard. Have children write on each construction paper card a consonant, digraph, or blend that can be added to the spelling pattern to form words. Attach the stack of letter cards to the posterboard using an "O" ring. Children can then flip through the book and practice the words in their word family. Finished flip books can be placed in a classroom learning center for individual practice by other children.

Word Family Rummy

SETUP: Gather 55 small index cards. Divide the cards into eleven piles of five cards each. On each card print five words from the same word family. You may wish to use the long- and short-*e* spelling patterns listed on page 45.

NUMBER OF PLAYERS: 2–4

OBJECT OF THE GAME: To collect five cards from the same word family and be the first player to have no remaining cards.

TO PLAY:
- Shuffle the deck of cards and deal each player seven cards. Place the remaining cards facedown in a "draw" pile. Turn the top card over to begin a discard pile.

- The player to the dealer's left begins play by choosing a card from either the draw deck or the discard pile. If the card drawn matches a word family in the player's hand, the player keeps that card and discards another. If the card drawn does not belong to a word family in the player's hand, the card can be discarded. A player may have no more than seven cards in hand at a time.

- The next player takes a card from the "draw" pile or the top card on the discard pile and discards the extra card. When a player gets all five cards from the same word family, the player removes them from his or her hand. These cards remain out of play.

- Play continues until one of the players has no cards remaining. This player is the winner and a new game can begin.

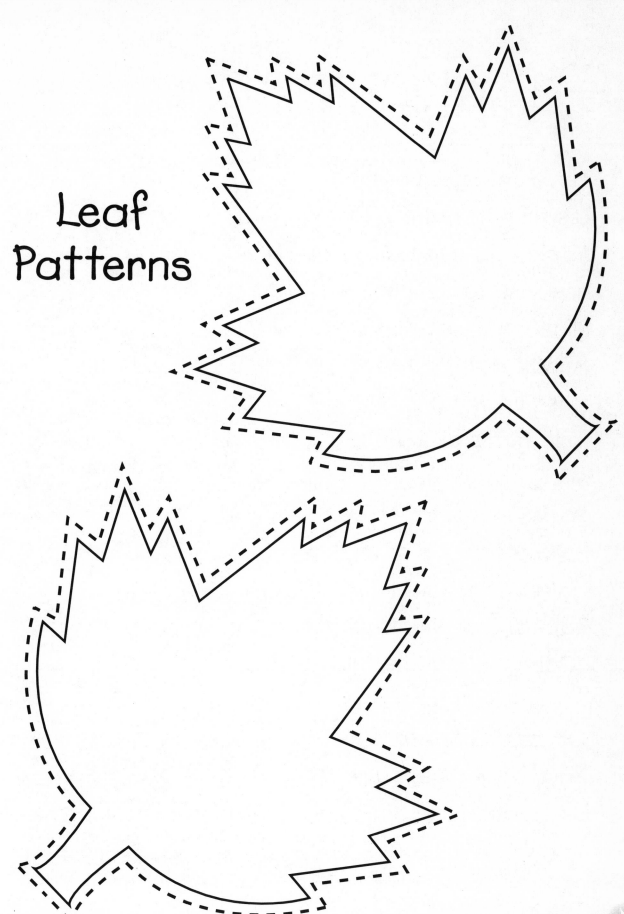

Leaf Patterns

Pumpkin Pie Time

Thanksgiving's coming.
It's time to bake pies.
Apple and pumpkin
are sure to delight!
Slice up the apples
(sneak a tiny bite)!
Mash up the pumpkin
(one that's plump and ripe).
Add a bit of sugar.
Sprinkle in some spice.
Roll out the pie crust.
Make it thin and light.
Bake the pies in the oven
'til they're browned just right.
Set them on the table.
Oh, they smell so nice!
Now, come one, come all
and bring your appetite!

by Dorothy Jean Sklar

Pumpkin Pie Time

Setup

● Photocopy the poem on page 48 for each child and write the poem on chart paper.

● Photocopy and cut out a pumpkin and pie pattern for each child.

Using the Poem

1 Distribute a pumpkin and a pie pattern to each child. Point out that the word *pie* contains /ī/. Then read aloud the poem. Explain to children that they are to hold up the pie picture every time they hear a word in the poem that contains the long-*i* sound. Repeat the procedure by pointing out that the word *pumpkin* contains /ĭ/. Reread the poem and have children hold up the pumpkin picture every time they hear a word that contains the short-*i* sound.

2 Then read aloud the following word list: *fish, bike, size, dig, five, fix, fight, hit, mix, lip, ride, right, tie, wig, wish, cry, mice, hill, lick.* If the word contains /ī/, tell children to hold up the pie card; if the word contains /ĭ/, they should hold up the pumpkin card. If children experience difficulties, extend the vowel sound in each word to emphasize it.

3 Ask children to identify the holiday when pumpkin pie is typically eaten. (Thanksgiving) Have children draw a picture of a Thanksgiving celebration. Suggest that they label any items in the picture whose names contain the long- or short-*i* sound.

SKILL

long and short vowel *i*

Materials

☼ chart paper
☼ markers
☼ pumpkin and pie patterns (page 51)
☼ scissors
☼ crayons
☼ drawing paper

Extending Learning

What Am I? Riddle Books

Have children create riddles for words with long or short *i*. For example, "I am cold and come in many flavors. Some people eat me in a dish and some people eat me in a cone. What am I?" (ice cream) To create the riddle books, have children write the riddle on a small sheet of paper and draw a picture of the riddle answer on another sheet of paper. Staple both sheets of paper onto a sheet of construction paper or oaktag. The riddle should appear on top of the drawing so that the riddle will flip up to expose a picture of the answer. Encourage children to share their riddles with classmates.

Group It!

Play a categories game with your class. Have children form teams of four. Then prepare a list of category cards (for example, foods, places, animals, clothes, famous people). To play, select a category card. Allow the groups two minutes to record on paper as many words as they can to fit the category. All answers must contain the long- or short-*i* sounds. Give one point to the team with the longest list of correct words. Give each team one point for each word that no other team has. Repeat this process with other categories. Play continues until one team earns 20 points.

Pumpkin and Pie Patterns

The More It Snows

The more it
SNOWS-tiddely-pom,
The more it
GOES-tiddely-pom
The more it
GOES-tiddely-pom
On
Snowing.

And nobody
KNOWS-tiddely-pom,
How cold my
TOES-tiddely-pom
Are
Growing.

by A. A. Milne

The More It Snows

Setup

● Photocopy the poem on page 52 for each child and write the poem on chart paper.

Using the Poem

1 Say the word *snow*, and ask children to identify the last sound in the word—/ō/. Then read aloud the poem "The More It Snows." Have children rub their arms as if they're cold every time they hear a word that contains the long-*o* sound. During a rereading, repeat the procedure with the word *top* and the short-*o* sound.

2 Have children generate words with long and short *o*. List these words in separate columns on the chalkboard.

3 Give each child a white paper circle and scissors. Show children how to fold the circle in half, then into thirds, and cut out random shapes along the folds. Tell them to be especially careful so that some of the fold remains intact. Then have children open the pattern to reveal the snowflake design. Once completed, have them write a long-*o* word on the front of their snowflake and a short-*o* word on the back.

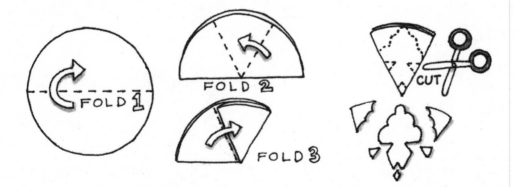

4 For a festive effect, let children decorate their snowflakes with glitter. Then tie pieces of string or yarn to each snowflake and hang from the ceiling or in a window to fill your classroom with sparkly snow. Encourage children to use the words on the snowflakes when writing stories or in their journals.

SKILL

long and short vowel *o*

Materials

※ chart paper
※ markers
※ white paper circles
※ scissors
※ crayons
※ string or yarn
※ glitter and glue (optional)

Poetry Corner

Curl up with a cup of hot cocoa and enjoy pcems about snowflakes, ice skating, snow angels, and other shivery wintry subjects in these two delightful poetry collections: *It's Snowing! It's Snowing!* by Jack Prelutsky (Greenwillow, 1984) and *Snowy Day: Stories and Poems* edited by Caroline Feller Bauer (HarperTrophy, 1986).

Create an *O* Word

Place the following letter card sets in individual envelopes: *oa, ow, o, g, s, b, t, s, l, f, r, c.* Ask children to work in pairs to make as many long- and short-*o* words as possible using the letter cards. Then have children record their words on paper. Award points for each correct word formed. Two-letter words are worth 1 point, three-letter words are worth 2 points, and words with four or more letters are worth 3 points. Continue with other letter card sets. For an additional challenge, limit the amount of time they have to form words. Slowly decrease the time as children become more skilled at using these and other letter combinations.

Build a Snowman

Play a snowy version of the game Hangman using words that contain long- or short-*o* sounds. First, prepare the twelve parts of the snowman using construction paper: Cut out three white circles for the snowman's body (one small, one medium, one large), two sticklike brown "arms," a black hat, a red scarf, one light-brown broom, a mouth, a nose, and two eyes. To play, gather children in a circle on the floor or at a table. Draw blanks on a piece of paper, one blank for each letter in the word. Have children guess a letter in the word. If correct, write the letter on the correct blank. If incorrect, add one body part to the snowman. Play continues until the word is guessed or the snowman is completed. Continue with other words.

Seed, Sprout, Flower

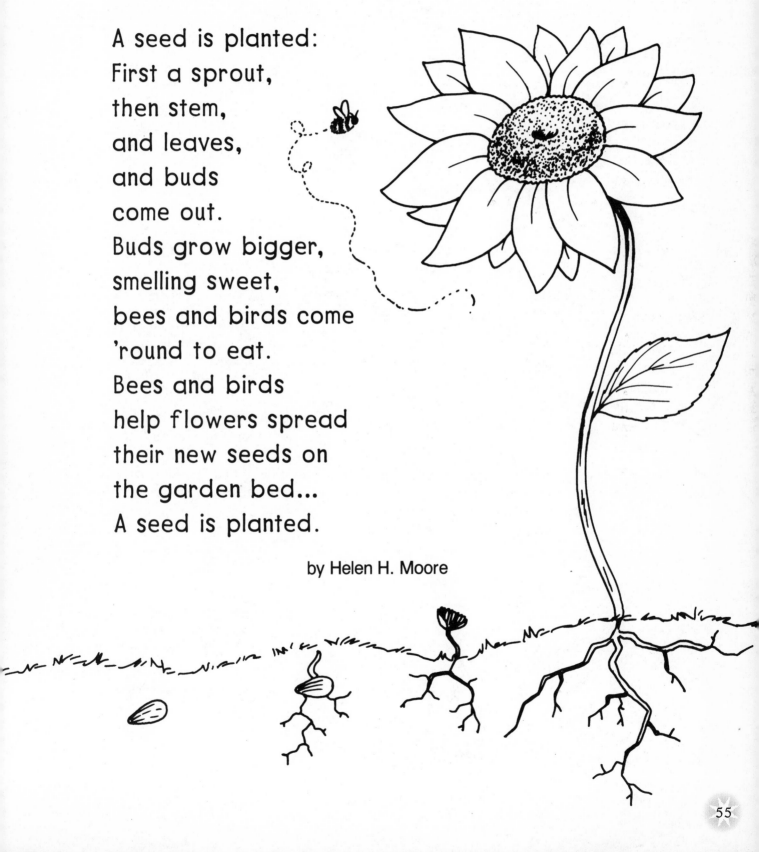

A seed is planted:
First a sprout,
then stem,
and leaves,
and buds
come out.
Buds grow bigger,
smelling sweet,
bees and birds come
'round to eat.
Bees and birds
help flowers spread
their new seeds on
the garden bed...
A seed is planted.

by Helen H. Moore

Seed, Sprout, Flower

SKILL

diphthong /ou/*ou, ow*

Materials

* chart paper
* markers
* flower pattern (page 58)
* scissors
* crayons
* crayons
* pencils

Setup

● Photocopy the poem on page 55 for each child and write the poem on chart paper.

● Photocopy the flower pattern page for each child.

Using the Poem

1 Read aloud the poem. Discuss with children the life cycle of a flower. You may wish to read aloud a book on this topic, such as *The Reason for a Flower* by Ruth Heller (Grosset & Dunlap, 1983).

2 Point out the /ou/ sound in the word *flower*. Have a volunteer underline the spelling that stands for this sound. (*ow*) Explain to children that the /ou/ sound can also be spelled *ou*. Have children search the poem for words with /ou/ spelled *ou*. (*sprout, out, round*) List these words on the chalkboard. Challenge children to add other /ou/ words to the list.

3 Explain to children that they will be creating /ou/ flowers. Hand out copies of the flower pattern page and ask children to write an /ou/ word on each petal. In the center, tell them to write *ou and ow words*. Afterward, invite them to lightly color the flower so that the words show through. Then have children cut out the flower and show them how to fold the petals inward, one at a time, so that they overlap. To make their flower bloom, children open the petals.

Rebus Stories

Challenge children to create rebus stories using /ou/ words. To begin, suggest a story title such as "The Clown," "Mouse Tales," or "The Golden Crown." Have children work with partners to write the story. When completed, have them select story words that can be replaced with rebus pictures. Then have them rewrite the story on large sheets of paper, replacing the selected words with rebus pictures. Place the completed stories in the classroom library.

Twenty Questions

Play a version of the game Twenty Questions with your class. To play, write an /ou/ word on an index card and tape it to a child's back. You may wish to use the words below. The child then walks around the room, asking different classmates yes/no questions to figure out the word. For example, if the word is *clown*, the child might ask, "Is this in the classroom?" "Is this an object?" "Is this an animal?" "Is this a person?" If your class hasn't had much practice asking questions, it is helpful to model question-asking before play begins.

Words with /ou/

clown	mouth	cow
owl	house	gown
flower	mouse	tower
towel	couch	crown
frown	cloud	brown

Flower Pattern

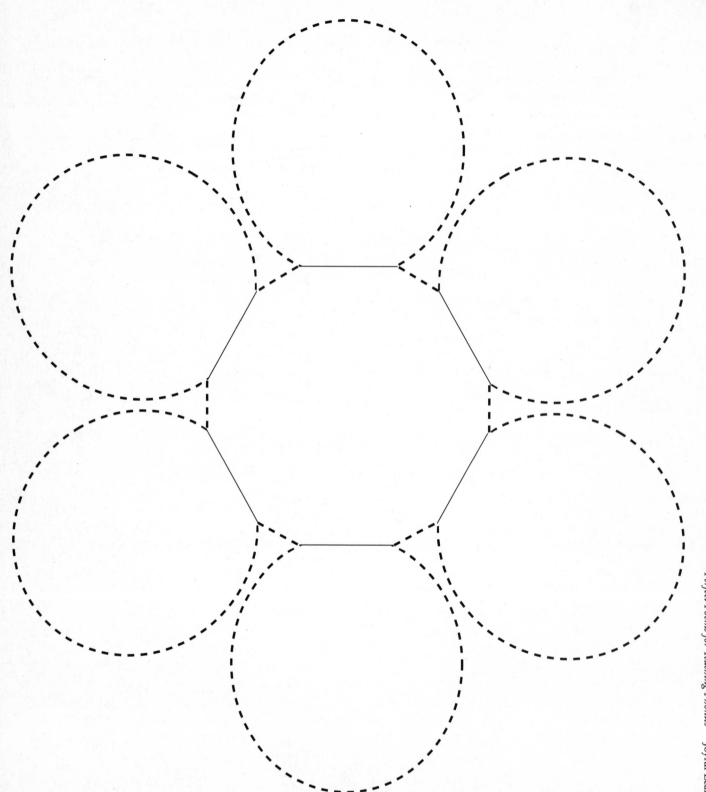

Perfect Poems for Teaching Phonics   Joyful Learning

Flashlights in the Dark

When darkness falls in summertime,
    The avenues of air
Are full of glowworm motor cops.
    They're zipping everywhere.

With flashlights snapping on and off,
    They signal Left! or Right!
Directing Bugland traffic jams
    On highways of the night!

by Frances Gorman Risser

Flashlights in the Dark

Materials

☼ chart paper
☼ marker
☼ index cards
☼ pencils or crayons
☼ flashlights
☼ tape

Setup

● Photocopy the poem on page 59 for each child and write the poem on chart paper.

● Write the following words on index cards: *summer, time, every, where, flash, lights, bug, land, high, ways.*

Using the Poem

1 Explain to children that you are going to read a poem about nighttime. This poem talks about glowworms. Ask children what a glowworm might be. Then read aloud the poem as children listen for clues to the glowworm's identity. When completed, discuss these poem clues. Then explain that glowworms are actually female fireflies—a kind of beetle. The abdomen, or stomach area, of a glowworm or firefly lights up and flashes on and off like a tiny flashlight. Continue by discussing what is real and what is make-believe in the poem.

2 Invite children to search the poem for compound words. Explain that compound words are words that are made up of two smaller words, such as *firefly* or *sunlight*. Then let children pretend to be glowworms! Darken the room, let volunteers shine a flashlight "glowworm" on each compound word, and flash on the two words that compose it.

3 Distribute the index cards. Challenge children to combine two cards to form a compound word from the poem. Continue using other compound base words and blank cards. For example, children can form compound words using common compound word parts such as *every, sand, snow, foot,* and *grand.* Have them add a word to each base word part to make a compound word. (See the Compound Base Words list on page 61.)

4 Let the glowworms go to work again! Have children tape their compound word pair cards to a bulletin board. Let them take turns shining the flashlight on each base word that makes up their compound, then shining the light on the entire word, and finally reading it aloud.

Compound Capture

Play Compound Capture. Make a large deck of base word cards that can be used to form compound words. You may wish to use the base words listed below. Divide the deck into two equal piles and place the cards facedown. To play, one child turns over a card from each pile. If the two cards form a compound word and the child can correctly pronounce it, the child keeps the cards. Play continues until no more words can be formed.

Compound Base Words

Pile 1		Pile 2	
air	cup	plane	cake
any	cow	thing	boy
back	every	yard	body
base	gold	ball	fish
tooth	star	brush	light
bath	home	room	work
bed	rail	time	road
birth	rain	day	bow
book	some	mark	day
sun	snow	set	man

Kooky Compounds

Challenge children to create original compound words, called "kooky compounds." To do this, provide several base words on index cards and have children create an original compound word by putting together two of the words in new ways. Some examples might include *rattlebird* or *starflower*. Invite children to illustrate and write a definition of their new kooky compound word. Display these on a bulletin board or compile into a class book.

Friends

Tall friends, short friends,
Skinny and wide;
Red haired, black haired,
Side by side.

Old friends, young friends,
And in-betweens;
Moms and Grandpas,
Tots and teens.

From Washington
To Delaware
Friends are found
Most anywhere.

by Janet C. Miller

Friends

Setup

● Photocopy the poem on page 62 for each child and write the poem on chart paper.

Using the Poem

1 Explain to your class that you are going to read a poem about friends. Provide time for volunteers to share the qualities of a good friend. Then read aloud the poem.

2 Have a volunteer point to the word *friends*. Explain to children that this word has one syllable. Point out that a syllable, or word part, has only one vowel sound. Clap one time as you say the word *friends*.

3 Next, point to the word *skinny*. Explain that the word *skinny* has two syllables, or word parts. Clap on each syllable as you say the word *skinny*. Repeat the same procedure with the three-syllable word *Washington*. Ask volunteers to select other words in the poem and tell how many syllables each has.

4 Have volunteers underline all one-syllable poem words, circle all two-syllable words, and draw a box around all three-syllable words. You may wish to provide children with other poems and repeat this procedure. For children experiencing difficulty, have them place their hand under their chin as they say a word. Point out that each drop of the chin signals a syllable.

SKILL

syllables

Materials

☼ chart paper
☼ markers

Poetry Corner

Could We Be Friends?, Poems for Pals by Bobbi Katz (Mondo, 1997) celebrates the joys and pains of friendship—from missing a friend who has moved away to sharing secrets with a special pal.

Use the following collections to share more haiku with children:

Cricket Never Does: A Collection of Haiku and Tanka by Myra Cohn Livingston (Margaret McElderry, 1997)

In the Eyes of the Cat: Japanese Poetry for All Seasons by Demi, translated by Tze-Si Huang (Henry Holt, 1992)

Syllable Sorting Circles

Write the following words on index cards: *rabbit, napkin, clap, book, circle, puzzle, fish, basketball, October, tiger, pilot, friend, turtle, bird, boat, bubble, little, grasshopper, photograph, triangle, mailbox, zero, carrot, umbrella, volcano, octopus, draw, spider, elephant.* Then make three yarn loops. Label the first loop "1 Syllable," the second loop "2 Syllables," and the third loop "3 Syllables." Have children sit in a circle around the yarn loops. Children then take turns selecting a word card, reading it aloud, and placing the card in the correct loop according to the number of syllables the word contains. If a child experiences difficulty, encourage others to provide assistance by clapping the number of syllables in the word.

Write a Haiku

Invite children to write a haiku. Explain that haiku is a Japanese poetry form. The poem contains three lines. Lines 1 and 3 contain five syllables; line 2 contains seven syllables. Write the haiku below on the chalkboard to provide an example. Gather the completed poems to form a class book.

Little ladybug
Busy working in my yard
Protecting my plants.